OF FLESH AND BONE

JOHN
FREDERICK
NIMS

RUTGERS UNIVERSITY PRESS
New Brunswick, New Jersey

OF
FLESH
AND
BONE

1 | FEW THINGS TO SAY

It's true, we write so little. Years between
Words in this, that, or the other magazine.
Few things to say—two maybe. Girls, know why?
You craze the air with pleasure. And you die.

The naked flesh brings tears: the ways so few
For love to enter. And its quick adieu.
Death, the cold ogler, shrugs—by many a way
Comes when the whim is on him. Comes to stay.

You bathers where the stinging sprays are blown,
Ponder your flesh, its queries on the bone.
A question mark, the calf. Thigh and yes there!—
Ponder the fond interrogations. Tear
Your gaze away to the spine's aplomb, rainbow
At shoulder. And flourish of hair, a jaunty "So?"
In teeth of the wind.
                    From time's old slapdash chasm
What drew (to abash the sky) that curious plasm?

Toe testing ocean, on the starlit sands
—Her body like brilliant reasoning—she stands;
And, blown with the blowing dark about her face,
Streamers (like fields of force from outer space),
Streamers: her love, grief, memory seem that tree
The northern lights shake glittering. Could we see,
We'd see all heaven cartooned, all myth aglow,
See nebulae shiver as she dips a toe.

"Living!" I grieved. "Each heartbeat, touch-and-go."
Sleepy, you touch and grin: "What touches, though!"

Flesh, buoyant flower, the sun's delight,
Love's clef and emblem, soon at night
These secrets joy kept close, the obscene
Black beetle, pain, go gloat between?

Black beetle? Gloat? The terms you choose!
As well say, pain the engraver 'd fuse
On steel each frailty.

                    Who'd suppose
Fire's of advantage to a rose?

It's brief and bright, dear children; bright and brief.
Delight's the lightning; the long thunder's grief.

These pretty students all the years!
The heart too often stumbles: none
But skirt the orchards worth a world.
Paths of the many. And the one.

Bored with that party, burrowing for the door,
Bored with time too,
When a girl, eyes lupine-blue not seen before,
Curls next to you—
Old lecher yet! No—say the rabbinical lore
So sears me through!
God lifts a hand on chaos. Lo, I soar
—*Loon!*—on the blue.

Good-byes were easy, with a casual hand.
But who, years later in a darkening land,
Seeing another with that same pale skin,
Fought with his heart to choke the blind tears in?

"No sense of age? These white hairs on your head,
You take this gold and pink thing to your bed?"
    Of age? For men, two sorts alone are doled:
    The dead years. The alive years, white or gold.
    I and the pink thing are alive-years-old.

This man on bended knee thanked God for much
Sweet manna from heaven—yet no sweetness such
As that two girls hated each other for his touch.

And yet a kiss (like blubber) 'd blur and slip,
Without the assuring skull beneath the lip.

Ten thousand cigarettes from now,
　　As many drinks away,
I may forget— "O honey, hush!
　　Let sleeping lovers lay."
Let sleeping lovers *lie*, my dear.
　　"I know as well as you.
But here's a love that's out for rhyme.
　　Can't even that be true?"

Here's homework, dear. Two verbs, *to lie, to lay.*
Before you lie forever, lover, say
What's the right use of each: *to lay, to lie.*
"One means *today,* dear teacher. One, *to die.*"

So, with one burning word from you
   Again the glacier came?
And where you set so cool a foot
   The world went up in flame?

"Now what a way to say you're cross
   But love me just the same!"

Some two decades, dear, apart,
Keep it shy, the younger heart?
Never mind. Some others passed
Bring us to one room at last.
Forty years we toss in two;
Forty thousand are too few
For the last triumphant bed—

"Hush and love me, winterhead!"

On your own flesh these fingers (once all thumbs),
My gold and ivory abacus, learned their sums.
The more I mused, the more assurance grew
What's loveliest, love, comes only *one*, or *two*.
Though some call *seven* holy, and some *three*,
I found no sevenish thing, no trinity.
Long at wit's end I wondered, *this?* or *this?*
Till all our *two*'s came single in the kiss.

May your flesh and its pleasant assembly delight
The many by day, but one only at night.
    "One only, my only, if only that one
    Would not look so broad by the girl-flushing sun."
Clay pigeons! I test me on every fine mark,
The better to find you, my dove, in the dark.
    "The better to lose me. Loose shooter, take heed.
    My pleasant assembly a bull's-eye indeed!"

"You say so, but will you be faithful? You men!"
But dear, I've been faithful again and again!

Sue said: Ridiculous sex! It calls and calls.
Cuckoo-clock frowzy on white marble walls.

"We met in error. If too close,
    Regrets. And I'm away.
Yesterday was easy come;
    Easy go, today.
Forget the way we burned, we two,
    That pain on either part.
Forget we fell convulsed as one."

    Said knifeblade to the heart.

Fresh from another's bed, that kiss for me?
Here's generous flesh, my dear? Soul's charity?
Or is the poor head puzzled? Good words run
Love one another. Not: *another one.*

"I'm Mark's alone!" you swore. Given cause to doubt you, I think less of you, dear. But more about you.

Helen, the tiny fire my fingers cup
Close to your breath—be careful. Don't look up.
Small gaudy fierce, it serves. But given a chance
Sheets of flame catch you in the tragic dance.

"For when we have blamed the wind, we can blame love."
Who'd blame the mindless wind? Sleepers that start
In fear when the ceilings heave like seas above?
Girls with their shattered dresden in the heart?

The world of shadow-matter science knows,
Those fabulous nations—we're the ghost of those?
Progress at last: the souls have room to move.
What gates in Eden scrape the aeruginous groove?

Some look at nature for the surface: eye
Vetch, vireo, pond with willow, wandering sky.
Dealers in scenery, no? Obscene as those
Who looking at a girl see only clothes.

Crude seeing's all our joy: could we discern
The cold dark infinite vast where atoms burn
—Lone suns—in flesh, our treasure and our play,
Who'd dare to breathe this fern-thick bird-rich day?

On sins, the deadly seven, these I thrive,
Hugging the hungry senses, the sweet five.
The soul can cope. The trick's keep flesh alive.

That blonde! waves lapping over rod and cone.
What glee in this amorous gadget, flesh and bone!

The flesh says: "Finish. I'm not long for you.
Tomorrow to another. And soon due
In ferns. Or on a gull's salt feather flown.
Or finswept shoalward. Finish. I'm a loan."

Now *Ban The Bomb!* I'm with you, though we fail.
Did *Ban The Arrow! Ban The Fist!* avail?
Still the red lips, ecstatic, cry "Ban! Ban!"
First ban yourself, sweet marcher. Banish man.

Men fought with axes, panting, nose to nose.
Women with pretty stitches pictured those.
The severed head lies beaming, "I'm a rose!"

Those tottering dead in Florida! Less obscene
Than neat geraniums in perpetual green?

When I've outlived three plastic hearts, or four,
Another's kidneys, corneas (*beep!*), with more
Unmentionable rubber, nylon, such—
And when (*beep!*) in a steel drawer (DO NOT TOUCH!),
Mere brain cells in a saline wash, I thrive
With thousands, taped to quaver out, "Alive!"—
God grant that steel two wee (*beep!*) eyes of glass
To glitter wicked when the nurses pass.

Once on the gritty moon (burnt earth hung far
In the black, rhinestone sky—lopsided star),
Two gadgets, with great fishbowls for a head,
Feet clubbed, hips loaded, shoulders bent. She said,
"Fantasies haunt me. A green garden. Two
Lovers aglow in flesh. The pools so blue!"
He whirrs with masculine pity, "Can't forget
Old superstitions? The earth-legend yet?"

Sweet flesh was shipped the bull-man once to eat.
You think it's changed, you children on the street?
Go home and pack. Tomorrow, off for Crete.

He scowled at the barometer: "Will it rain?"
None heard, with all that pattering on the pane.

Three rattlers sank their fangs in Dr. Crudd.
"Thank *you*," he bowed. "It much improves the blood."

Once Cruddy in the countryside
Touched poison ivy. And it died.

"A dead tradition! Hollow shell!
Outworn, outmoded—time it fell.
Let's make it new. Rebel! Rebel!"
Said cancer-cell to cancer-cell.

"The famous bard, he comes! The vision nears!"
Now heaven protect your booze. Your wife. Your ears.

"New clarity hailed in poet P. B. Clutter!"
True: the old mumble's made almost a mutter.

He lectures, palms extended on the air,
Much like the pope to bless St. Peter's Square.
Heaps laurel on his bumpy brow benign;
Chants, "Acres of Parnassus, and all mine!"

"You told her, that thing in the dress,
I heard you, a disgusting *Yes.*
And yet—you can't have meant it so—
Once to a noble cause said *No.*"
  I? The old dizzy whiskey, rhyme,
  Made me see double at the time.

Honors corrupt the blood. Disturb like gin.
We squirm being flattered, cringe being told, "You're in!
About your brow the immortal auras glow!"
Liar! I sniff the festering blood below.

Let chips of marble fly, and chisel chime:
His life was meager, but his song sublime.

"His song was *what?*" You heard me. For the rhyme.

Once, lovely Chloe here asleep in clay
Warmed with warm flesh whatever place she lay.
And now so long abed, yet cold as stone?
And—so unlike our Chloe—sleep alone?

Lie light on the light lady, somber loam.
She's much converted now; keeps to one home.

The whole world takes her to its bed below.
As she took all the world. Or nearly so.

Death, to see that puffy shade,
Grins, relaxing on his spade.
His work, rot the fair and true.
If effluvium's any clue,
That's the one thing you could do.
Death the expert whistles low:
"Purer rot I've none to show!"

I see you, love, in your low home
The night-things comb. And catacomb.
"A sort of trash, the body." No:
Good sticks to set the soul aglow.
"Good sticks?" In dark of midnight, think:
To brighten truth, we blacken ink.
"Mere image!" God's Quijote swore
The passionate bed's mere metaphor.

And what of this: "The soul in its rose-mesh"?
Yet ordure sweetens long before dead flesh.

How all these cheeks a-twitch, loose, dumpy, dull,
Long for the echoing splendors of the skull.

Last year I'd tease, "So beautiful? So dumb?"
She'd laugh "I guess," and let the tears half come.
"Confuse such easy lines?" "I tried and tried!"
"Julie, you moon at school. All dreamy-eyed!"
    So last year. Now, as girls lie on the sand
    In summer, hair flung over cheek on hand,
    She—by the curb, in pink of flares. Poor head,
    Lost in your dreams? Confuse *Early to bed?*

In traffic shuddering as it shied too near
That tumble of lovelocks at the silent ear,
She lay, outstretched as if for pleasure, more
Languid than any girl on any shore.
Love taught the pose. *Such cronies, love and death?*
Old bosom friends. If differing, by a breath.

Night by night the bony mesh
Slumbered in its bed of flesh.
Now the bone, turned out of bed,
Wanders the wide night instead.
Not a miser picks at gold
As these shabby nails the mold.
Ah, to patch it, shank and girth,
There's not earth enough on earth.

I loved a girl. She died. I stood here, so;
Stared at the something strangers put below.
Again I stand a moment. Not to stay.
Evenings she'd tease, "Don't wait if I'm away."

And here the two by the one grievance haunted
Lie in the dark. But not the dark they wanted.

The flesh, when crisp as snow and tulip, takes
Its color from corruption: all life through
Feeds on the death of fields, of fin and wing. And
Taints, like the bitter gruel on which it grew.

Life, that struck up his cocky tune with *breath*,
Finds, to conclude in music, only *death*.

INDEX